Be a Good Sport!

by Jennifer Waters

Content and Reading Adviser: Mary Beth Fletcher, Ed.D.
Educational Consultant/Reading Specialist
The Carroll School, Lincoln, Massachusetts

Spyglass
BOOKS

 COMPASS POINT BOOKS

Minneapolis, Minnesota

Compass Point Books
3722 West 50th Street, #115
Minneapolis, MN 55410

Visit Compass Point Books on the Internet at *www.compasspointbooks.com*
or e-mail your request to *custserv@compasspointbooks.com*

Photographs ©: Bob Krist/Corbis, cover; Richard T. Nowitz/Corbis, 4; Reuters NewMedia Inc./Corbis, 5;
Jennie Woodcock/Corbis, 6; James A. Sugar/Corbis, 7; Visuals Unlimited/Mark E. Gibson, 8;
Kit Houghton/Corbis, 9; Two Coyotes Studio/Mary Foley, 10, 13; Stephanie Maze/Corbis, 11;
Duomo/Corbis, 12, 14; AFP/Corbis, 15; Bill Schild/Corbis, 16; Jerry Cooke/Corbis, 17;
S. Carmona/Corbis, 18; Todd Gipstein/Corbis, 19.

Project Manager: Rebecca Weber McEwen
Editor: Heidi Schoof
Photo Selectors: Rebecca Weber McEwen and Heidi Schoof
Designer: Erin Scott, SARIN creative
Illustrator: Anna-Maria Crum

Library of Congress Cataloging-in-Publication Data

Waters, Jennifer.
  Be a good sport! / by Jennifer Waters.
      p. cm. — (Spyglass books)
Summary: Introduces the concept of sportsmanship, providing examples of
proper behavior while playing team sports.
Includes bibliographical references and index.
  ISBN 0-7565-0375-2
1. Sportsmanship—Juvenile literature. [1. Sportsmanship.] I. Title.
II. Series.
  GV706.3 .W38 2002
  796—dc21
                                2002002541

Contents

Good Sport!

Sports can be fun.
They are even more
fun if everyone is
a good sport.

Do you know how to be
a good sport?

Adults who help each other are
good sports.

Fair Play

You can follow the rules
and be fair.
A good sport knows the
rules and does not *cheat*.

If people do not follow the rules
in karate, they can get hurt.

Safety First

You can play safely.
A good sport makes sure
that no one gets hurt.

In this race, riders have to be
careful of their horses, too.

Other Players

You can be nice to any other players. A good sport makes the game fun for everyone.

Good sports say "Good luck!"
before a race.

People in Charge

You can listen to
the *coach* or referee.
Good sports know these
people will help them
stay safe and have fun.

A referee helps players
follow the rules.

On Your Side

You can help your teammates. A good sport cheers for teammates when they do well.

Hockey players in the *Paralympics* cheer after a good play.

Sometimes You Win

You can be a good winner.
A good sport is nice
to the losing team.

These girls race each other and
are still friends.

Sometimes You Lose

You can be a good loser.
A good sport has
good *manners*, even if
the other team wins.

A good sport shakes hands with
the other team after the game.

Sporting Facts

In *professional* sports, players often get traded to other teams. If they are not good sports, they might have to play with people who are mad at them!

In a *martial arts* contest, each person bows to the other before a match. This shows they will fight fairly.

Glossary

cheat–to disobey the rules

coach–a person who teaches and helps athletes or sports teams

manners–rules that help people be kind and polite

martial arts–sports that were invented to help people protect themselves

Paralympics–sports competitions that happen every four years for people with physical challenges

professional–when somebody plays a sport to make money

Learn More

Books

Gibbons, Gail. *My Soccer Book.* New York: HarperCollins, 2000.

Jeunesse, Gallimard, and Pierre-Marie Valat. *Sports.* New York: Scholastic, 1998.

Kuklin, Susan, *Hoops with Swoopes.* New York: Hyperion Books for Children, 2001.

Web Sites

www.printablechecklists.com/checklist38a.shtml

www.youth-sports.com/

23

Index

GR: G

Word Count: 142

From Jennifer Waters

I live near the Rocky Mountains,
but the ocean is my favorite place.
I like to write songs and books.
I hope you enjoyed this book.